© Aladdin Books Ltd 1991

*First published in
the United States in 1991 by*
Gloucester Press
387 Park Avenue South
New York NY 10016

Design: Rob Hillier
Editor: Catherine Bradley
Picture Research: Emma Krikler
Illustrator: Ron Hayward Associates

Library of Congress Cataloging-in-Publication Data

Pimlott, John. 1948-
    Middle East : a background to the conflicts /
John Pimlott.
      p.cm.--(Hotspots)
    Includes index.
    Summary: Examines the background of the
present crisis in the Middle East precipitated by
Iraq's invasion of Kuwait: and discusses the Arab-
Israeli conflict and the search for a solution to the
Palestinian problem.
    ISBN 0-531-17329-1
    1. Iraq-Kuwait Crisis, 1990- --Juvenile literature.
    2. Israel-Arab conflicts--Juvenile literature.
    [1. Iraq-Kuwait Crisis, 1990- 2. Israel-Arab
conflicts.] I. Title. II. Series.
    DS79.72.P56 1991
    956.704'3--dc20   91-2673 CIP   AC

Printed in Belgium

The front cover shows the Kuwaiti border on
January 17, 1991.

The back cover shows Palestinian refugees in
Jordan.

The author, Dr. John Pimlott, is the Deputy Head
of War Studies at the Royal Military Academy at
Sandhurst, England. He is the author of several
books on the Middle East.

The consultant, Dr. Timothy Niblock, is a lecturer
in politics at the University of Exeter, England.

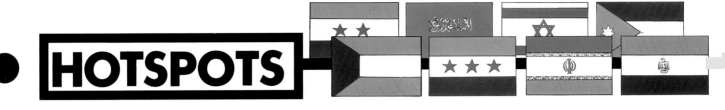

HOTSPOTS

MIDDLE EAST
A BACKGROUND TO THE CONFLICTS

JOHN PIMLOTT

A GLOUCESTER PRESS BOOK

Contents

▷ Allied forces celebrate the
liberation of Kuwait City,
February 27, 1991. Seized by
the Iraqis in early August 1990,
the city – devastated by nearly
six months of occupation – was
the main objective of Operation
Desert Storm, masterminded by
U.S. General Norman
Schwarzkopf.

Introduction

On February 27, 1991 U.S. President George Bush declared a cease-fire in the war against Iraq. The war had proved a military triumph. It had been provoked nearly seven months earlier by the Iraqi invasion of Kuwait. Since January 16, bombers had pounded targets in Iraq and Kuwait around the clock. Then in a mere 100 hours, American, Arab, British, French and other forces had swept into southern Iraq and Kuwait, with authority from the United Nations. Kuwait was liberated and an Iraqi army of 330,000 men in Kuwait was destroyed.

However, a military victory is worth little unless the peace settlement that follows is effective. In the search for a solution the international community faces intractable problems. The Middle East, important in terms of oil and world trade, has always attracted outside powers, such as Britain, France, the United States and the Soviet Union. This external pressure often worsens local conflicts. Following the Gulf War, the rest of the world has to find a way to prevent a repetition of Iraq's aggression. It must also address the other, deep-rooted conflicts in the area.

Saddam Hussein, the president of Iraq, attacked neighboring Kuwait primarily for its oil wealth, which he wanted to use to help Iraq recover from a bitter eight-year war against Iran. The dispute between Iran and Iraq dates back centuries. The United Nations immediately condemned the invasion and Saddam Hussein tried to widen the conflict by declaring a "holy war" against Western interference, and by linking any withdrawal from Kuwait to an Israeli withdrawal from the West Bank and Gaza, which Israel occupied in 1967. Israel had been established as a separate state in 1948 on what had been the Arab land of Palestine, and has long rejected any such withdrawal on the grounds of security. Any Middle East peace settlement will probably have to include some sort of Arab guarantee that Israel be allowed to exist, in exchange for Israel permitting a Palestinian Arab state to be established on the West Bank and Gaza.

The Middle East's problems are so deeply entrenched and the region is so important to the world's economy, that it is virtually impossible for the Middle Eastern countries to find their own solutions. Outside powers that intervene encounter a host of local conflicts – Arab against Arab, Persian against Arab, Arab against Jew. The chances of a settlement of these conflicts are slim.

The roots of conflict

The Middle East has long been a center of trade and ideas, producing new cultures, religions and rivalries. After 1918 Britain and France controlled much of it.

The term "Middle East" is a European one, dating back to times when areas of the world were described according to their distance and direction from London or Paris. Denoting a region stretching from Egypt in the west to Iran in the east, and from Turkey in the north to Yemen in the south, the Middle East has suffered from interference by outside powers.

There are a number of reasons for this. One is its position as a land bridge linking Asia, Europe and Africa. The Middle East has always been a center for trade – an area in which camel trains met and markets were established. Moreover, as traders converged, they brought with them ideas, out of which new forms of civilization and religion developed. The Middle East contains shrines belonging to three of the most influential religions of the world – Judaism, Christianity and Islam. The latter, following the teachings of the Prophet Muhammad in the 7th century A.D., led to a flowering of Arab culture, language and government.

The decline of the Islamic Empire, which stretched from Spain, through North Africa and the Middle East, deep into central Asia, created a vacuum which outside powers sought to fill. These included European states, eager to spread Christianity during the Crusades and control the trade routes to the Middle East. By the early 16th century the Turks ended up ruling the region, establishing the Ottoman Empire.

△ The *Kaaba*, or shrine, is in the center of the Grand Mosque in Mecca. Muslim pilgrims must circle the shrine seven times and kiss and touch the Black Stone built into the eastern wall to gain forgiveness for their sins.

▷ The Suez Canal was opened on November 17, 1869. Built by French engineers under Ferdinand de Lesseps, the canal was a major strategic waterway from the start, halving the journey time from Europe to the Far East. The countries with Far Eastern empires, such as Britain and France, saw the canal as vital.

4

European expansion

Some 350 years later Ottoman weakness led to a more widespread European presence. In 1869 French engineers completed the Suez Canal, linking the Mediterranean to the Red Sea through Egyptian territory. Its existence cut the sailing time from Europe to the Far East by half. European powers with interests in the Far East – principally France and Britain – felt that they needed to control both the canal itself and its approaches. The French already had a controlling interest in the Suez Canal Company (to which all ships using the waterway paid tolls), but when the ruler of Egypt sold his shares, Britain was quick to snap them up.

It was a prelude to an Anglo-French scramble for territory around the canal, which the British won. In 1878 they gained Cyprus from the Turks and four years later established control of Egypt. Cyprus was a useful base from which to monitor traffic approaching the canal from the north. In 1898 Sudan was added, extending British rule down the west bank of the Red Sea. At about the same time the port of Aden was developed and part of Somaliland seized, covering both sides of the Bab el Mandeb straits, where the Red Sea joins the Indian Ocean. Britain also managed to get a toe-hold in Kuwait on the Persian Gulf. The French only managed to grab Djibouti, opposite Aden, and part of Somaliland.

World War I and after

In 1914 Turkey joined Germany and Austria-Hungary in their war against Britain, France and Russia. During World War I (1914-18), British and Empire troops fought the Turks in Gallipoli, Mesopotamia (Iraq) and Palestine. The French, intent on defeating the Germans in Europe, contributed little, although this did not prevent a secret Anglo-French agreement (the 1916 Sykes-Picot Agreement) about the breaking up of the Ottoman Empire, once the fighting was over. Despite British promises to the Arabs of independence, it was the secret agreement that was put into effect after the war.

By the Treaty of Sèvres in 1920, the Ottoman Empire was divided up. Some areas received a degree of independence, and in 1932 Saudi Arabia emerged as a unified state. The majority of Arab lands were given as mandates from the newly established League of Nations to Britain and France, on the understanding that they would prepare them for eventual self-rule. In the process, the European concept of a "state system" was imposed on the area. Britain received Palestine, Transjordan and Iraq, while the French gained "Greater Syria" (which became Syria and the predominantly Arab-Christian Lebanon). The new states were alien to their populations. The European powers then tried to ensure friendly rule by installing members of the Hashemite family as rulers, and trouble quickly broke out. Neither Syria nor the Hijaz (Western Arabia) accepted the arrangement.

The growth of Arab nationalism

This combination of Turkish defeat and European interference strengthened the sense of Arab nationalism in the Middle East. The ideal was a return to the pan-Arabism of the Islamic Empire, in which all Arabs (and perhaps all Muslims) would come together in a single, powerful entity. However, loyalties to the state began to grow and there were religious splits.

Ever since early Islamic times, Islam had been divided into two main sects. These sects had their origin in a dispute over the succession to the prophet Muhammad, between the followers of the prophet's father-in-law Abu Bakr (who became the Sunnis) and those of the prophet's cousin and son-in-law Ali (the Shi'ites). Differences of practice and belief developed between the two groups. Rivalry often arose between the Shi'ites and Sunnis in the newly created states.

△ Jewish women pray at the Wailing Wall in Jerusalem, a symbol of their faith. Reputedly the last remaining part of Solomon's Temple, destroyed by the Romans in the aftermath of a Jewish revolt in 70 A.D., the wall came under Israeli control during the Six-Day War in 1967.

▷ These are members of a Bedouin tribe, photographed in Kuwait. The Bedouin are the indigenous people of large parts of the Middle East, especially Arabia and Jordan. Traditionally nomadic, dependent for their livelihood on trade and camels, many tribes have now adapted to oil, modernization and wealth. There are still important communities of Bedouin in some Arab countries, and they retain many traditions, especially their strong Muslim faith.

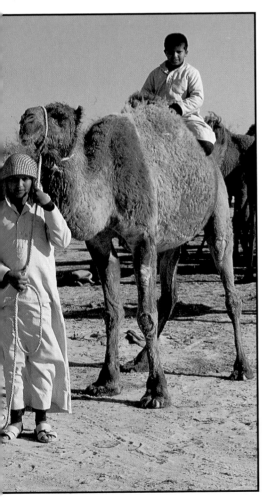

The Jewish problem

This was not the only cause of rivalry. It was soon revealed that during World War I, Britain had promised to support the creation of a Jewish homeland in the mandated territory of Palestine, where the Biblical state of Israel had existed. In November 1917, Arthur Balfour, Britain's foreign minister, sent a letter to the World Zionist Organization promising that his government would "view with favor" the establishment of a Jewish homeland. However, if Jews were to be allowed to settle in Palestine, Arabs would suffer and might revolt against the British.

In the end, the British had an interest in conciliating the Arabs. One of the reasons for this was because Britain needed oil and all the major oil fields in the Middle East were in Arab territories. Oil had been discovered (principally in Mesopotamia and Persia) at the beginning of the 20th century, and it was a vital raw material for British industry. Britain did not want to alienate the Arabs. However, the Arabs remained deeply suspicious of Jewish immigration and the loss of Palestinian land. They blamed Britain for allowing Jewish settlers to displace the Palestinian Arabs. By 1920 there were more than 800,000 Arabs and less than 70,000 Jews in Palestine. The scene was set for future conflict.

The Arab-Israeli conflict

Since 1948 both Jews and Arabs have fought over Israel's right to exist and the Palestinians' right to a homeland. Israel has lost over 16,000 people while the Arabs have lost ten times that number.

The Zionist dream of an independent state of Israel became reality on May 14, 1948, as British troops pulled out of Palestine. The mandate had proved impossible to administer fairly and it had been referred back to the United Nations (the successor to the League of Nations, known as the UN) in April 1947. Eight months later, the UN voted for a partition of Palestine into Arab and Jewish areas: it was the Jewish area – constituting Galilee in the north, a coastal strip around Tel Aviv in the center and the Negev desert in the south – that became the state of Israel.

It was lucky to survive. On May 15, 1948 armies belonging to five Arab states – Lebanon, Syria, Iraq, Jordan and Egypt – launched attacks into Palestine seeking to restore the territory to the Palestinians by force. The Israelis fought hard, defeating a series of poorly coordinated Arab attacks and taking advantage of UN-imposed cease-fires to recover and redeploy. By January 1949, the immediate threat was over, but the Arab powers refused to recognize the right of Israel to exist. The rift between the two sides deepened, particularly as more than 725,000 Palestinians had fled to neighboring countries – acting as a constant reminder of Arab failure.

△ Jewish immigrants arrive in Israel, late May 1948. They were leaving Europe after "the Holocaust." Nazi Germany exterminated six million Jews during World War II.

The militarization of Israel

Israel's problems were not over. In geographic terms, the new state was weak, for despite some territorial gains during the "War of Independence," it lacked easily defendable borders and was vulnerable to attack. In addition, Israel had a Jewish population of only 650,000, which was easily outnumbered by the millions of surrounding Arabs. Israel's economy was weak, it lacked natural resources and, once the Egyptians closed the Suez Canal to Israeli shipping, it had no easy access to world markets. Later on, the construction of a port at Eilat gave access to the Gulf of Aqaba. However, the Egyptians could easily close the Strait of Tiran.

In such circumstances, it would have been advisable for Israel to seek peace by negotiating with its neighbors. Arab governments insisted, however, that Palestinian refugees be allowed to return to their homes. The Israeli government refused to agree to this. The Israelis developed a distinct "strategy for survival" based on military success. Able-bodied Jews were conscripted into the Israeli Defense Force (IDF) at the age of 18 to receive military training before returning to civilian life as reservists, available in the event of war to boost the size of the IDF. Mobilization of reservists was expensive – whenever it occurred, the Israeli economy would grind to a halt. Also Israel could not afford to lose many of its soldiers, so this meant that military operations had to be short. They also had to be decisive, defeating enemy armies before they invaded Israel, and they had to aim to capture territory which could be used either to improve the security of Israel or to trade for promises of peace.

This strategy depended on good intelligence about enemy intentions so that the IDF could be mobilized in time to carry out a preemptive attack. It was first used in October 1956 against Egypt as part of an Anglo-French and Israeli assault. Gamal Abdul Nasser, President of Egypt, had seized the Anglo-French Suez Canal Company. This triggered a military response from Britain and France. They agreed with Israel – fearful of Egypt's growing political and military power – that it invade Sinai, between the Negev and the Suez Canal, while they attacked the canal itself. The Israeli assault went well. Catching Egyptian troops by surprise, IDF paratroopers seized the Mitla Pass in western Sinai and were quickly joined by armored units from the Negev. Israeli forces were on the east bank of the canal in less than four days.

▽ A Palestinian Arab family waits to be evacuated to the Gaza Strip in March 1949, having fled from the fighting between Arab armies and the new state of Israel.

9

U.S. backing for Israel

The victory could not be exploited. American pressure forced the British and French to abandon their campaign and, in March 1957, the Israelis had to withdraw, making way for a UN peacekeeping force in Sinai. It was then that they added a further refinement to their strategy – the need for a superpower backer who would not only provide economic support, but would also, in any future war, step in to organize a cease-fire at the moment of maximum IDF success, leaving Israel in possession of enemy territory.

Such a backer was not difficult to find. At the time the two world superpowers that counted were the United States and the Soviet Union. Since the end of World War II they had been engaged in a rivalry to increase their influence worldwide, known as the Cold War. Nasser was already receiving aid from the Soviet Union, and the United States proved willing to provide Israel with technology, money and weapons. It could also give Israel support in the UN where, as a permanent member of the Security Council, the United States could veto anti-Israeli resolutions. Arab powers, aware that their dispute with the Jews had now become part of the superpower stalemate, felt increasingly frustrated.

△ Arab leaders meet in March 1957, four months after the Anglo-French and Israeli attacks on Egypt: second from left is King Hussein of Jordan; second from right is the Egyptian leader, Gamal Abdul Nasser.

Israel's vulnerability
In the north, Galilee was overlooked from the Golan Heights in Syria, while the West Bank of the Jordan river dominated the coastal strip and the thin Jewish link with Jerusalem. Further south, the Negev had long open borders with Jordan and Egypt, while the Gaza Strip pointed like a finger straight at Tel Aviv.

10

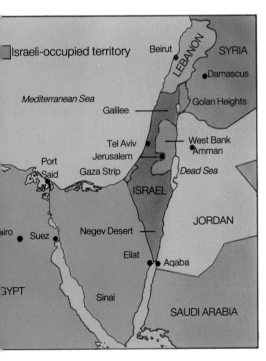

△ Israel's borders show the areas seized and retained in 1967 – the Gaza Strip, the West Bank and the Golan Heights. The Sinai was evacuated in 1979.

The Six-Day War

This did not mean that the Arab countries gave up the fight for Palestine. Nasser, regarded as a hero by many Arabs for his defiance of Britain and France in 1956, tried to create Arab strength by bringing together the various states. In 1958 he organized a union between Egypt and Syria – the United Arab Republic (UAR) – and forged links with King Hussein of Jordan. His aim was to surround Israel, exerting such pressure on Israel that it would be forced to make concessions. In May 1967, after Egyptian units moved into Sinai, Nasser asked for the removal of the UN peacekeeping force. War seemed inevitable and the Israelis triggered their "strategy for survival."

It worked. Early on June 5, Israeli aircraft attacked airfields throughout Egypt. Similar attacks followed on airfields in Jordan, Syria and western Iraq: by the end of the day, over 300 Arab aircraft had been destroyed, mainly on the ground. This enabled Israeli armored units to advance into Sinai free from air attack, smashing through Egyptian defenses before moving swiftly to block the eastern end of the Mitla Pass, trapping Nasser's army. The Egyptians collapsed, losing over 800 tanks, and by June 8, most of Sinai was in Israeli hands. At the same time, a campaign was conducted against the Jordanians on the West Bank, by the end of which (June 7) the Israelis had seized control of the West Bank, including Jerusalem. Finally, on June 9-10 the Syrians were ousted from the Golan Heights. UN-sponsored cease-fires ensured that the Israelis were left occupying nearly 67,000 square kilometers (26,000 square miles) of Arab territory.

Resolution 242

As a result of the Six-Day War, Israel was an easier country to defend – Galilee was no longer overlooked from the Golan Heights, the threat to the coastal strip had been lifted and Sinai could now act as a buffer against future Egyptian attack – but the Arabs had been deeply humiliated. At the UN, Resolution 242 was passed, calling on Israel to give up the occupied territories, but there was no real pressure on the Israelis to comply.

Indeed, many Jews regarded the West Bank and Jerusalem as theirs by historical right and had no intention of withdrawing. Compromise was impossible and force seemed the only option on both sides – for the Israelis, to protect their enlarged state; for the Arabs, to reverse the outcome of 1967.

11

The success of their strategy in 1967 made the Israeli leaders feel complacent. Some Israelis believed that all they had to do was to repeat the process to guarantee victory – but this was foolish. Israel was still surrounded and, in certain key respects, weak. Many Arabs, recognizing Israeli strength in conventional military terms, supported guerrilla warfare as a way of undermining the Israeli hold on the occupied territories. The Palestine Liberation Organization (PLO) had, in fact, been formed in 1964, but it took the Six-Day War and the appointment of Yasser Arafat as chairman to transform it into a coherent force. Guerrilla attacks on Israel itself began in the late 1960s and soon spread to targets abroad, including aircraft, embassies and non-Israeli Jews.

▷ Yasser Arafat has been Chairman of the Palestine Liberation Organization since 1969. Arafat has adopted a variety of methods to regain Palestinian land, ranging from "armed action" to global diplomacy. Despite defeat in Lebanon in 1982 and ill-judged support for Iraq in 1990-91, Arafat still represents the Palestinians.

△ Israeli troops push deep into Egypt, having crossed the Suez Canal on October 15/16, 1973. Their advance, made in response to an Egyptian attack into Sinai ten days earlier, seemed to threaten Cairo and the future of Egypt. A UN cease-fire was hastily arranged, coming into effect on the 24th to end the October War.

Nasser recognized as early as 1967 that if the Israelis could be forced to fight long wars, their economy would suffer, leading them to seek peace on Arab terms. He therefore initiated a War of Attrition, sending helicopters and commandos across the Suez Canal into Sinai to make sure that the Israelis maintained mobilization and suffered a steady drain of casualties.

In response, the Israelis mounted counterattacks which, by 1970, involved air strikes close to Cairo, forcing the Americans to step in to halt this. Soviet-supplied surface-to-air missiles (SAMs) were deployed by the Egyptians to some effect, suggesting that Israeli air power could be countered. When Sagger antitank missiles were also made available by the Soviets, the Israeli strategy for survival began to be seriously undermined.

The October War

Nasser died in 1970. His successor, Anwar el-Sadat, tried to draw the United States into mediating a settlement. When the United States showed itself to be reluctant, Sadat decided to use force. By 1973 he had held secret meetings with President Hafez al-Assad of Syria and, on October 6, both Arab powers attacked Israel. Egyptian forces, protected by SAMs, crossed the canal with unexpected speed, destroying sandbanks on the Israeli side by using high-pressure hoses to wash them away before bridging the waterway with Soviet-supplied pontoons. Israeli aircraft sent to intervene were shot down, while armored counterattacks fell victim to the Saggers.

Meanwhile, Syrian units moved onto the Golan Heights, pushing the Israelis back. In a separate move, designed to force Western powers to reconsider their support to Israel, Arab members of the Organization of Petroleum Exporting Countries (OPEC) raised the price of oil on the world markets and announced a boycott on the export of oil to states supporting Israel. This produced economic chaos in many Western countries.

Israel recovered and, using new tactics, managed to counteract the SAMs and Saggers. By October 11, 1973 the Syrians had been defeated and, when the Egyptians moved deeper into Sinai two days later, Israeli forces destroyed them. This enabled the Israelis to counterattack across the canal on October 16, threatening Cairo and surrounding an entire Egyptian army. For a time it looked as if the Soviets might intervene (causing the Americans to order a nuclear alert), but a UN cease-fire ended the fighting on October 24.

▽ President Anwar el-Sadat of Egypt (left) and Prime Minister Menachem Begin of Israel (right) sign the Camp David agreement, put together by President Jimmy Carter (center) in 1978. The following year a full peace treaty was signed between Egypt and Israel, ending 30 years of hostility. It was a significant breakthrough.

The Camp David agreement

The war had lasted 18 days and had considerably weakened the Israeli economy. More significantly, American support for Israel had now to be tempered with the new reality of the "oil weapon." The Israelis themselves recognized that their strategy was flawed and had to change. Thus when Sadat, facing economic problems of his own, decided to open direct contacts with Israel, he found a ready response in both Tel Aviv and Washington.

President Jimmy Carter invited Sadat and the Israeli prime minister, Menachem Begin, to Camp David in 1978, where a settlement was reached. A peace treaty followed in March 1979, whereby Egypt recognized Israel's right to exist in exchange for an Israeli withdrawal from Sinai. The PLO and other powers condemned the agreement.

Lebanon's civil war

By 1979, the PLO was widely recognized as representing the Palestinian people, but it had suffered various setbacks in its campaign against Israel. In 1970 King Hussein had thrown the PLO out of Jordan, because he was afraid of a Palestinian takeover of his state. The PLO and its allies had moved to Lebanon, only to find themselves caught up in a civil war between the conservative Christian government and the mainly Muslim opposition movement. In 1976 Syria, intent on avoiding instability on its doorstep and wary of a strong Muslim government emerging in Beirut, intervened in Lebanon, pushing Muslim and PLO forces toward the Israeli border. The PLO did not recover until the early 1980s, when a new campaign against Israeli interests abroad and against settlements in northern Galilee was mounted. With Egypt no longer a threat, the Israelis felt free to invade southern Lebanon, on the face of it to push the PLO back, but actually to destroy it for good.

It was a poor move. Although militarily Operation Peace for Galilee succeeded – in six days (June 6-11, 1982) Israeli units reached Beirut and defeated Syrian forces in the Beqa'a Valley – politically it created more problems than it solved. President Ronald Reagan, preoccupied by Britain's war in the Falklands, refused to sponsor a UN cease-fire, leaving the Israelis to fight on for six weeks before local arrangements were made.

△ Palestinian women view with despair the aftermath of the massacres, carried out by Christian militias affiliated to the Israeli Army, at Sabra and Chatilla, just to the south of Beirut, September 1982. Worldwide disgust led to condemnation of Israeli actions in Lebanon.

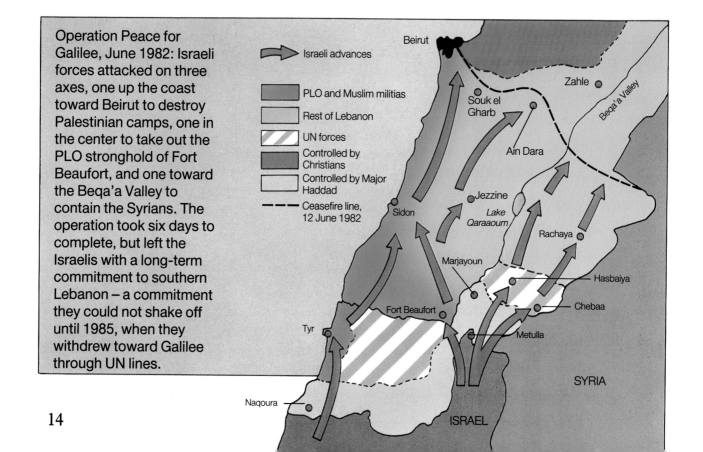

Operation Peace for Galilee, June 1982: Israeli forces attacked on three axes, one up the coast toward Beirut to destroy Palestinian camps, one in the center to take out the PLO stronghold of Fort Beaufort, and one toward the Beqa'a Valley to contain the Syrians. The operation took six days to complete, but left the Israelis with a long-term commitment to southern Lebanon – a commitment they could not shake off until 1985, when they withdrew toward Galilee through UN lines.

Israeli advances

PLO and Muslim militias

Rest of Lebanon

UN forces

Controlled by Christians

Controlled by Major Haddad

Ceasefire line, 12 June 1982

Beirut

Zahle

Beqa'a Valley

Souk el Gharb

Ain Dara

Jezzine

Lake Qaraaoum

Sidon

Rachaya

Marjayoun

Hasbaiya

Chebaa

Fort Beaufort

Tyr

Metulla

Naqoura

SYRIA

ISRAEL

Most of the PLO withdrew from Beirut under international supervision, but the fighting did not end. Indeed, Israel lost considerable international support when it emerged that Christian militia units operating with the IDF deliberately massacred Palestinian families in camps at Sabra and Chatilla in September 1982. In the end, it took the Israelis until 1985 to extricate themselves from Lebanon, having suffered over 600 dead for very little long-term gain.

The *Intifada*

In the aftermath of Lebanon, Israel suffered both economically and politically, particularly when many Western states adopted a more balanced approach to the Arab-Israeli dispute because of oil. This was shown in the near-success of a peace plan put forward in 1986 by King Hussein, involving the creation of a Palestinian "homeland" in the West Bank and Gaza Strip, under Jordanian protection, once the Israelis had withdrawn. It only failed when the Americans refused to sanction Soviet involvement in a peace conference and the Israelis, predictably, refused to talk to the PLO.

World anger then increased over Israeli actions in the West Bank and Gaza against the Palestinian uprising known as the *Intifada*. By the late 1980s, Israel was in danger of being isolated, especially since world attention shifted away from the Arab-Israeli dispute toward the second major crisis area in the Middle East – the Gulf.

△ Palestinians demonstrate against Israeli rule in the West Bank during the early stages of the *Intifada*, December 1987. Israel's response to the unrest was brutal, doing nothing to gain world sympathy: even the Americans have condemned the repression, despite their commitment to Israel.

The MNF
In September 1982 the United States, France and Italy (joined later by Britain) sent troops to Beirut to prevent further fighting. The Christian Lebanese government used them as a shield to move against Muslim militias. The Muslims retaliated and bombed the U.S. and French headquarters in October 1983, killing 297 soldiers. The job of the Multi-National Force (MNF) became impossible, leading to withdrawal in February 1984.

The Iran-Iraq War

The most damaging and costly war in recent years was the Iran-Iraq War of 1980-88, in which an estimated 900,000 people died.

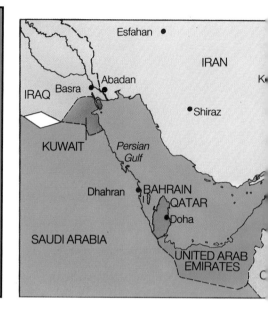

The Gulf states – Iran, Iraq, Kuwait, Saudi Arabia, Bahrain, Qatar, the United Arab Emirates and Oman – are split along ethnic, religious and political lines, producing crises and wars. Relations between Iraq – the former Turkish-ruled territory known as Mesopotamia, covering an area around the Tigris and Euphrates rivers – and Iran (formerly Persia) have long been poor. The border between the two states, running from Turkey in the north to the tip of the Gulf in the south, represents the meeting of Arabs and Persians. In addition, since the Islamic split of the 7th century A.D., the Persians have tended to adopt Shi'ite beliefs while the mainly Shi'ite Arabs in Iraq have been ruled by Sunnis.

The effects of such differences may be seen in the development of the two states. Iraq, like many of its neighbors in the Arab part of the Middle East, was an artificial creation, carved out of the Ottoman Empire by Britain and France in 1920. It contained within its borders a host of different Arab groups, split between Shi'ite and Sunni sects. In the north and northeast the ethnically distinct Kurds harbored deep nationalist feelings, and demanded an independent state for themselves.

This made Iraq a difficult state to govern and, although the Hashemite dynasty installed by the British survived, it was never popular. Overthrown in 1958, it made way for a nationalist, republican government intent on stressing its independence from foreign powers, particularly those of the West, by now alarmed at the growing Soviet influence in the Middle East.

△ The map shows the various countries on the Persian (or Arabian) Gulf. Because of its oil, the Gulf has been a conflict area for over a decade.

▽ The War Memorial in Baghdad represents the two halves of a broken heart. With over 150,000 Iraqis killed in the war with Iran, it is apt.

△ Shah Muhammad Reza Pahlavi was the supreme ruler of Iran from 1941 to 1979. His reign, with its mixture of Westernization and repression, did much to trigger the fundamentalist revolution of early 1979, bringing to power the Ayatollah Khomeini. Fabulously wealthy, the Shah died of cancer in Cairo in 1980.

The Ba'athists take over

Internal disputes and poor relations with neighboring states – in 1961, for example, Iraqi military moves toward the newly independent emirate of Kuwait were only stalled by the swift commitment of British forces to the northern Gulf – did little to ensure political stability in Iraq, where a series of coups and countercoups occurred. It was not until July 1968, when power was seized by members of the socialist Ba'ath party, that order was imposed.

The Ba'athists consolidated their hold on the state through a combination of economic concessions, principally to Shi'ite dissidents in the south, and ruthless repression. By the early 1970s Iraqi society had been transformed, with Ba'athist political cells ensuring loyalty to the government in Baghdad, and this enabled the country to exploit its oil power. Military forces were given new, modern equipment, chiefly supplied by the Soviet Union (with whom Iraq negotiated a treaty in 1972), and this resulted, inevitably, in opposition from the West, especially the United States.

Iran's modernizing policy

The American reaction was to increase its support to more "moderate" powers in the region, including Saudi Arabia and the smaller Gulf states but concentrating on Iran. A long-established independent country, with its own distinctive culture, Iran had been ruled by Shah Muhammad Reza Pahlavi since 1941. He was keen to modernize Iran, using his immense oil revenues (Iran was the world's fourth largest producer of oil) to Westernize the state. He turned to American advice and bought up-to-date technology, including weapons from the West.

This caused some internal opposition, particularly from those Shi'ites who regarded the Shah as someone who was taking the people away from strict Islamic beliefs. However, by the early 1970s the country was widely regarded as the most powerful in the Gulf region, if not in the Middle East as a whole.

As such, in Western eyes, it acted as a block to Soviet expansion and a counter to socialist, pro-Soviet regimes, such as that in Baghdad. The Shah's repressive policies, carried out by his secret police throughout Iran, were conveniently ignored. With Iran and Iraq effectively on opposite sides of the superpower divide, and bearing in mind the well-established religious and ethnic differences between the two states, friction was inevitable.

It manifested itself over the Kurds, whose demands for independence from Iraq had developed into the open revolt of the Kurdish Democratic Party (KDP). Opposition to Iraqi rule had been apparent for years – the KDP was founded as early as 1946 – and successive Iraqi governments had attempted to make concessions, but a compromise based on a Ba'athist promise of autonomy within Iraq rather than full independence had failed. By 1974 a virtual civil war had broken out, during which the recently reequipped Iraqi Army made some headway. In response, the Shah of Iran, grasping an opportunity to weaken his neighbor (and to quiet Kurds living in Iran), provided the KDP with artillery, surface-to-air missiles and even troops. The Kurds went on the offensive, "liberating" up to 64,700 square kilometers (25,000 square miles) of Iraqi soil.

The border dispute

The Iraqi government, thoroughly alarmed, offered Iran concessions in exchange for the withdrawal of support from the KDP. The concessions were over disputed border territory, particularly the Shatt al Arab waterway, linking the Gulf to the Tigris and Euphrates rivers.

During the era of British influence, in 1937, a treaty had established the border between Iran and Iraq along the eastern bank of the Shatt al Arab, giving Iraq control of the waterway. This meant that Iranian oil tankers had to ask Iraqi permission, employ Iraqi pilots, and even fly the Iraqi flag. Iran demanded that the border should be moved to the middle of the waterway (the *thalweg*) so as to allow Iranian ships free passage along the eastern channel. Successive governments in Baghdad refused to negotiate – until 1975. At a meeting in Algiers, Iranian and Iraqi delegates agreed to a settlement: if the Iranians would stop supporting the Kurds, the Iraqis would accept the *thalweg* as the new international border.

In one sense, the Iraqis gained – the agreement allowed them to turn on the now isolated Kurds and crush the revolt – but in another it was a potential disaster, making the Ba'ath party look weak in the eyes of the Iraqi people. Saddam Hussein, leader of a younger, more militant group within the party, searched for an opportunity to reverse the Algiers Accord, conscious of the humiliation that its signing had represented. In July 1979, as a preliminary move, he engineered the "resignation" of the existing president of Iraq and took his place.

▽ Saddam Hussein is the ruler of Iraq. He rose through the Ba'ath Party to gain power in 1979, since which time he has fought two wars, with substantial losses to his country.

18

◁ Kurdish guerrillas strike an aggressive pose. With a burning desire for independence, coupled to an intimate knowledge of terrain in northern Iraq, the Kurds make ideal guerrilla fighters, but their fortunes have been mixed. Close to success in 1975, they suffered as a result of the Algiers Accord. In 1991 they faced the full force of Saddam Hussein's army following the Gulf War. The Iraqi Army's tanks and helicopters demolished Kurdish opposition.

▽ The Ayatollah Khomeini returns to a tumultuous welcome in Tehran, February 1979. In exile since 1964, the Ayatollah – a deeply respected Islamic cleric – acted as a focus for unrest in Iran, gaining power in the aftermath of the Shah's downfall.

The Iranian revolution

By then, Iran was in chaos. Reforms introduced by the Shah, particularly after 1977 when United States President Jimmy Carter asked for improvements in human rights, had alienated many of his more traditionalist subjects, particularly those belonging to the Shi'ite sect. They looked for inspiration and leadership to the Ayatollah Ruhollah Khomeini, an influential cleric who had been in exile since 1964, chiefly in Iraq then, and after the Algiers Accord, in France. The first of a fresh wave of anti-Shah demonstrations in January 1978 was in response to a government-inspired press campaign against the Ayatollah Khomeini. By September over 100,000 people were on the streets of Tehran.

As might be expected, the government reaction was brutal – on September 8, 1978 over 5,000 demonstrators were killed when troops opened fire – but this served merely to inflame the situation. Protest escalated until, on January 16, 1979, the Shah and his wife fled into exile. On February 1, the Ayatollah Khomeini flew into Tehran to a rapturous welcome. The government which the Shah had left in place was finally overthrown 10 days later.

Fundamentalism in action

Divisions soon appeared among the revolutionaries, especially when it became apparent that the Ayatollah and his followers were aiming to create a strict, fundamentalist Islamic republic. At the same time, in an attempt to stifle pro-Shah support, the armed forces were purged, with many officers being executed and units disbanded. At this point, the United States – alienated in November 1979 when Islamic fundamentalists seized the American embassy in Tehran, holding more than 50 diplomats hostage – withdrew its support from Iran. This left the country isolated and, more significantly, short of spare parts for the weapons purchased by the Shah. An American rescue mission – Operation Eagle Claw – failed miserably in April 1980, but the hostages were eventually freed in January 1981 in exchange for an American agreement to release Iranian assets frozen in November 1979.

The outbreak of war

All this seemed to play into the hands of Saddam Hussein. His avowed enemy had been transformed into a weakened country ruled by clerics dedicated to the creation of a strict Islamic regime, and to the spread of fundamentalism into Shi'ite areas of southern Iraq.

In contrast, the Iraqi armed forces, fresh from their campaigns against the Kurds, were strong and reasonably well-equipped with Soviet-designed weapons. The time seemed ripe for a sudden attack on Iran, designed to restore the pre-1975 border along the Shatt al Arab and to seize the oil refineries at Abadan and Khorramshahr. On September 22, 1980, after a series of contrived border clashes, the Iraqis invaded Iran.

At first, all went according to plan. Khorramshahr fell after heavy fighting and Iraqi units threatened both Abadan and the oil-rich Iranian province of Khuzestan (containing a predominantly Arab population which, it was felt in Baghdad, would be quick to rise against the Ayatollah), but the success did not last. The regime in Tehran did not disintegrate under the pressure. In fact, there was a surge of Iranian nationalism: air force pilots and military weapons technicians returned voluntarily from exile to fight against the traditional enemy, after the Ayatollah declared a *jihad* (holy war) against the "unbeliever" Saddam Hussein. There was a steady flow of recruits into the Revolutionary Guard, an elite formation willing to sacrifice itself in battle.

△ The Iranian oil refinery at Abadan was damaged during an Iraqi air raid in September 1980. The Iraqis laid siege to Abadan, but failed to take it.

▽ This map of the Iran-Iraq War 1980-88 shows the border between the two states. Most of the fighting took place in the northern and southern parts of the war zone.

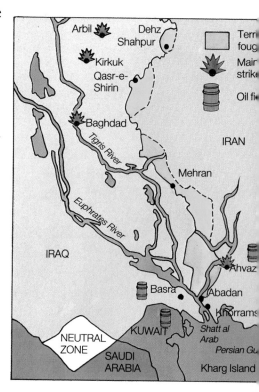

▽ This scene from the Iran-Iraq War, February 1984, shows the results of a conflict that had degenerated into a stalemate: against a backcloth of flames and smoke, soldiers – both of them badly wounded – seek shelter in dugouts. By 1987 the Iraqis had suffered over 150,000 dead, compared to more than 600,000 Iranians.

Stalemate

The Iraqi offensive stalled, enabling the Iranians to mount a counterattack which, in 1981, recovered much of the lost ground. To complicate matters further for Saddam Hussein, on June 7, 1981 – in an action separate from the war – Israeli aircraft destroyed a nuclear reactor outside Baghdad. Israeli politicians claimed that such an attack was essential in order to prevent the development of an Iraqi nuclear weapon that might be used against Tel Aviv.

The war between Iran and Iraq quickly degenerated into a stalemate which neither side seemed able to break. Iranian offensives, spearheaded by fanatical fundamentalists who attacked in "human waves" regardless of casualties, gained some success. In May 1982 they cleared Khorramshahr of Iraqi occupiers and advanced toward the Tigris River in Kurdistan in the north, but they failed to achieve a decisive victory against Iraqi defenses and artillery bombardments.

For a time, it did look as if Iraq might be defeated economically rather than in battle – the fighting closed the Shatt al Arab to Iraqi shipping, cutting off oil exports from Iraq through the Gulf. Saddam Hussein survived by calling for aid from other Arab powers, many of which feared a spread of Islamic fundamentalism from Iran. By 1988, it was estimated that Saddam Hussein had received subsidies totaling $60 billion from the Gulf states. He used the money to reequip his armed forces. Special Republican Guard units were raised and given weapons received from the Soviet Union and Western Europe, such as Exocet sea-skimming antiship missiles from France.

The war grinds on

The Exocets were used to hit Iranian oil tankers and installations in the Gulf in an attempt to cripple the Iranian economy. Saddam Hussein hoped this would force Iran to seek peace. At the same time, air attacks began on Iranian cities, including Tehran, which were to be supplemented in 1987-88 by strikes using Soviet-designed Scud missiles. The Iranians responded in kind, escalating the war to new levels of destruction. The superpowers – the United States and the Soviet Union – remained aloof, fearing the consequences of victory by either side, although U.S. warships were eventually used to escort Kuwaiti oil tankers, carrying Iraqi cargoes, to deter Iranian attacks.

Meanwhile, the ground war continued without a major breakthrough by either Iran or Iraq. Each year, Iranian Revolutionary Guards and young conscripts (some only 12 years old) threw themselves against Iraqi defenses. In 1984 they seized the important oil-producing area of Majnoon Island and two years later, in a surprise attack, captured the Fao Peninsula – cutting Iraq off from the Gulf entirely – but suffered horrendous casualties.

Saddam Hussein tried to play for time by authorizing the use of chemical weapons, which was illegal according to international law. Then in 1987 the Iraqi Republican Guards used new tactics to defeat an Iranian attack on Basra. The Iranians were drawn into deep defensive positions before being destroyed by artillery and Republican Guard counterattacks. By then, the war had cost an estimated 600,000 Iranian and 150,000 Iraqi lives.

▽ Iranian women receive weapons training, November 1986. Although clearly a propaganda photograph, designed to shock Muslim and world opinion by showing an uncharacteristic scene, it does typify the impact of the Iran-Iraq War on the societies of both combatant countries: under the pressure of "total" war, even the most sacred beliefs have to be questioned and overturned.

△ Women and children are evacuated from the Kurdish village of Halabja, March 1988. Halabja was the scene of a deliberate gas attack by Iraqi forces as they moved into Kurdistan during the final battles of the Iran-Iraq War. Up to 500 people were asphyxiated: an atrocity which raised fears of Iraqi chemical weapons during the Gulf War of 1990-91.

The peace settlement

It proved too much for Iran. By early 1988, United States aircraft and warships were more directly involved in the Gulf, hitting Iranian oil platforms. On July 3, 1988, the United States shot down an Iranian airliner, thought to be an attack aircraft heading for the USS *Vincennes*, killing 290 passengers and crew on board. In addition, Iran was short of allies and isolated. Only Iraq's enemies Israel and Syria, each for different reasons fearful of a victorious Iraq, had offered any support. The Ayatollah's government searched for a settlement through the United Nations and, on July 18, 1988, a cease-fire was finally agreed.

Saddam Hussein hailed it as a crushing Iraqi victory, although in reality the war had been crippling. Iraqi forces were able to recover both Majnoon Island and the Fao Peninsula during the final offensives in early 1988, but the Iraqi economy was in ruins. At the same time as Iraqi forces were fighting the Iranians, they were also settling old scores with the Kurds. A reported 500 people were killed by gas in the Kurdish village of Halabja.

One of the consequences of the Iraqi victory was that Saddam Hussein put himself forward as a great Arab leader who had saved the Gulf from Islamic fundamentalism. Many of his wartime "allies" hastily reassessed their support. Iraq suddenly seemed dangerous: Saddam Hussein might seek to expand his territory to gain oil and influence. Events in 1990 were to show how true such an analysis was. The instability resulting from the Iran-Iraq War helped create the Gulf crisis and conflict of 1990-91.

◁ The use of chemical weapons (gas) was perhaps the most shocking aspect of the Iran-Iraq War. Saddam Hussein, using technology provided by Western firms, had established a number of chemical-warfare factories in Iraq. His forces used gas shells, fired by artillery, on a variety of occasions, both to shock and, sometimes, to survive what could otherwise have been certain defeat. Iranian forces had to take precautions, including (as shown here) using respirators and antigas clothing.

23

The Gulf War

Iraq's invasion of Kuwait produced a devastating response from the US-led coalition, but regional problems are not yet solved.

Early on August 2, 1990, Iraqi forces invaded Kuwait, announcing that they were supporting an internal Kuwaiti revolt against the ruler, Sheikh Jaber Ahmed al-Sabah. Despite a buildup of Iraqi troops along the border over the previous few days, the attack caught the rest of the world by surprise. Within hours, most of Kuwait was in Iraqi hands and, six days later, Saddam Hussein declared that it was no longer an independent state, but the "19th province" of Iraq.

Saddam's motives

The crisis had begun on May 28, 1990, when Saddam Hussein – desperate for an oil price rise as a way of raising money in the aftermath of his war with Iran – accused some countries of deliberately keeping prices low through overproduction. On July 18 he followed this with the more specific accusation that Kuwait had stolen Iraqi oil by slant drilling across the border; he demanded compensation and cancelled all repayments of loans received from Kuwait, said to total over $10 billion. The Kuwaitis were prepared to negotiate, but when Saddam Hussein went further on August 1, claiming the Kuwaiti islands of Bubiyan and Warba for Iraq, it was obvious that little could be achieved. Twenty-four hours later, the invasion took place. The Kuwaiti Army could not stand up to such an onslaught and the ruling emir and his family fled to Saudi Arabia.

△ An Iraqi armored personnel carrier comes under heavy fire from members of the Kuwaiti Army as the capital, Kuwait City falls to the invading Iraqis, August 2, 1990.

Resolutions 660 and 661

World reaction was swift. Led by the United States, the West condemned Iraq, freezing its financial assets, suspending trade and halting all weapons shipments to Baghdad. In addition, the UN Security Council passed Resolution 660, demanding an immediate Iraqi withdrawal. For once, with relations between the superpowers relatively cordial and the Soviet Union obsessed with its own internal problems, U.S. proposals in the UN were not vetoed, giving President George Bush virtually a free hand. On August 6 the UN accepted Resolution 661, imposing a trade embargo on Iraq (whereby all UN members agreed not to do business with Saddam Hussein), and two days later the first U.S. troops arrived in Saudi Arabia. Their mission was to defend the Saudi kingdom against further Iraqi aggression, but as forces from other countries – notably Britain, France, Italy, Egypt, Syria and the smaller Gulf states – were also committed, something more active was possible.

▽ U.S. troops move into the Saudi Arabian desert as part of Operation Desert Shield – the response to Iraqi aggression in Kuwait. Many units came from the United States.

Operation Desert Shield

While these forces, operating under the codename Desert Shield, were being deployed – a lengthy operation, with men and supplies having to travel thousands of miles – more peaceful methods of persuading the Iraqis to leave Kuwait were pursued. King Hussein of Jordan tried to negotiate a settlement in mid-August; Saddam Hussein merely used the opportunity to widen the crisis, offering a withdrawal from Kuwait if the Israelis agreed to pull out of the West Bank and Gaza Strip. The Americans saw this as a ploy to lure anti-Israeli Arab states away from the developing coalition, and refused to negotiate. This was not Saddam Hussein's only miscalculation.

On August 16 he ordered U.S. and British nationals in Kuwait to be rounded up and taken to Iraq, eventually to act as human shields around economic and military targets that might be bombed. In a change of heart, Saddam released all women and children by the end of the month.

Meanwhile, the Desert Shield buildup continued, with U.S. warships, aircraft and ground units moving to the Gulf in what was now clearly intended to be a liberation of Kuwait by force if negotiations failed. Other coalition powers followed suit – in September, for example, the British government sent armored units from Germany, after U.S. satellite photographs showed Iraqi troops digging in on the Saudi-Kuwait border.

The hostage issue

But the coalition was unlikely to attack as long as the remaining hostages were still in Iraqi hands, and their release took priority. On October 1, President Bush hinted that a Middle East peace conference, at which the Palestinian question would be discussed, might occur if Saddam Hussein withdrew from Kuwait, and this, together with Soviet pressure on Baghdad for a peaceful outcome to the crisis, persuaded the Iraqi leader to soften his stance.

On November 15, he offered to accept Bush's proposal, but refused to pull out of Kuwait first. Sensing weakness, the Americans increased the pressure: on November 29, UN Resolution 678 called on Iraq to release all remaining hostages immediately and to withdraw from Kuwait by January 15, 1991, otherwise force would be sanctioned. On December 6 Saddam Hussein, clearly trying to compromise, let the hostages go.

It was a major error, freeing the allies to use force to liberate Kuwait (and weaken Iraq so that future aggression would be impossible) without risking death or injury to their own people. Negotiations continued right up to the deadline – on January 9, 1991 U.S. Secretary of State James Baker met with Iraq's Foreign Minister, Tariq Aziz, in Geneva – but to no avail. Saddam Hussein refused to withdraw from Kuwait without gaining any concessions.

The military buildup

By then, 465,000 allied troops from 28 countries, fielding 3,500 tanks and 2,000 artillery pieces, were in place, backed by 1,700 land-based and 480 naval aircraft. They faced an estimated 535,000 Iraqis in or close to Kuwait (a figure later amended to 330,000), deployed in a "sword and shield" defense: any coalition assault into Kuwait would have to fight through the border fortifications (the "shield"), upon which it would be counterattacked by Republican Guard tank units (the "sword"). It looked like a very tough proposition.

But the Americans and their allies, commanded by General H. Norman Schwarzkopf, had no intention of attacking the enemy head on. Instead, they planned to use air power, with its highly accurate bombs and missiles, to weaken Iraq and cut off its forces in or around Kuwait before launching a ground assault. When the UN deadline expired on January 15 with no sign of an Iraqi withdrawal, Schwarzkopf was ready to transform Desert Shield into Desert Storm.

△ The scene over Baghdad on January 16, 1991 as Desert Shield becomes Desert Storm: U.S. and allied aircraft attack military-associated targets in and around the Iraqi capital.

▽ General H. Norman Schwarzkopf, commander of U.S. forces in Saudi Arabia, attends a press conference in January 1991. He was responsible for planning and executing the liberation of Kuwait.

Air power

Beginning on January 16, American, British, French, Italian and Arab aircraft, plus naval cruise missiles (designed to follow contour-hugging routes to hit precise targets), flew deep into Iraq. Their impact was immediate and devastating. Surface-to-Air Missile (SAM) sites were hit, Iraqi aircraft were destroyed on their runways and special "strike packages" of fighter-bombers, backed by Stealth fighters (built to penetrate enemy radar screens without being seen) and B-52 bombers, ranged far and wide. The attacks – many using laser and TV-guided bombs – continued for 40 days and nights, during which Iraq's radio and TV systems were destroyed, along with electricity power stations, command bunkers and industrial sites thought to be associated with nuclear and chemical-weapon manufacture.

The Scud missile attacks

The Iraqi Air Force put up little opposition – within two weeks most of it had been destroyed or had fled to Iran – although Saddam Hussein did launch Soviet-designed Scud missiles into Israel and Saudi Arabia. His intention seems to have been to widen the war. If, as a result of the attacks, Israel joined in, any Israeli strikes on Iraq would threaten to split the coalition, leading Arab states to reconsider a commitment that entailed fighting on the same side as Israel. As it happened, U.S. Patriot SAMs and unexpected Israeli restraint prevented escalation, but for a time the allied air forces were sidetracked into fairly fruitless hunts for mobile Scud launchers.

▽ Tel Aviv, the recognized capital of Israel, comes under attack by Iraqi-launched Scud missiles, February 1991. Saddam Hussein hoped to draw Israel into the Gulf War, but failed.

Targetting the army

By early February Iraq was suffering under the aerial bombardment. Allied aircraft diverted their attention and began to hit bridges and roads linking the forces in Kuwait to Iraq itself. At the same time, Republican Guard units to the southwest of Basra, together with the frontline shield in Kuwait, came under sustained aerial attack.

Saddam Hussein searched for a way out, offering concessions via the Soviets, but Bush responded with a new ultimatum: the Iraqis were to begin to leave Kuwait by February 23, or face the consequences of a ground assault. Schwarzkopf's plan was to tie down Iraqi forces in Kuwait while U.S., French and British armored and airmobile units swept through southern Iraq in an outflanking move, cutting Kuwait off by advancing to the Euphrates River.

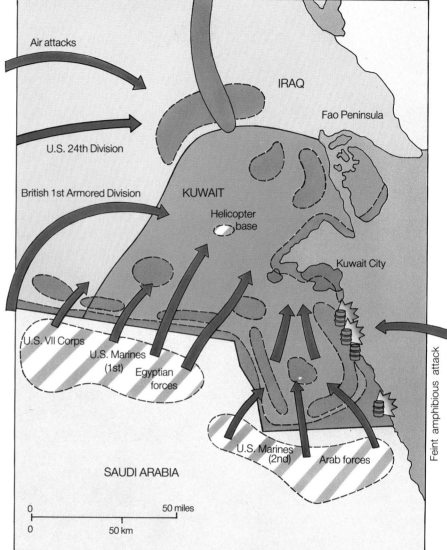

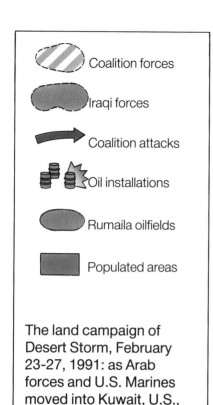

Coalition forces

Iraqi forces

Coalition attacks

Oil installations

Rumaila oilfields

Populated areas

The land campaign of Desert Storm, February 23-27, 1991: as Arab forces and U.S. Marines moved into Kuwait, U.S., French and British armored and airmobile units executed a left-hook attack, designed to cut behind the main Iraqi defenses and trap the occupying army. It was more effective than many anticipated.

Air attacks

IRAQ

Fao Peninsula

U.S. 24th Division

British 1st Armored Division

KUWAIT

Helicopter base

Kuwait City

U.S. VII Corps

U.S. Marines (1st)

Egyptian forces

U.S. Marines (2nd)

Arab forces

SAUDI ARABIA

Feint amphibious attack

0   50 miles

0   50 km

The land offensive

Schwarzkopf's plan worked brilliantly. On February 23, Arab forces and U.S. Marines pushed north into Kuwait, meeting little coherent opposition, while coalition tanks further west broke into Iraq. By then, Iraqi units were demoralized and isolated: they surrendered in droves. On February 27, after a ground campaign lasting a mere 100 hours, Bush halted the attack. At a cost of 140 allied dead, Kuwait had been liberated and up to 100,000 Iraqis killed.

Saddam Hussein agreed to a cease-fire, accepting all UN resolutions, but his problems were not over. In the next few weeks he faced civil war in Iraq, as Shi'ite dissidents in the south and Kurds in the north tried to seize territory. The coalition refused to intervene, hoping that by leaving the Iraqis to sort out their own problems, it could not be accused of imposing a settlement.

△ Symbols of Saddam Hussein's defeat in Kuwait: lines of Iraqi soldiers, demoralized by weeks of air attack, surrender to allied units. Up to 200,000 Iraqi troops gave themselves up.

▽ Although Saddam Hussein's forces were comprehensively defeated in Kuwait and southern Iraq, the after effects of the Gulf War will be felt for years. As they retreated, Iraqi troops deliberately set fire to Kuwaiti oil wells, filling the atmosphere with flames, smoke and toxic gases.

The future

This may turn out to be a mistake, for any attempt at creating lasting peace in the Middle East stands little chance of success as long as Saddam Hussein remains in power. Kuwait is in ruins, beset with oil fires and internal troubles and the peace in other Gulf states has been disrupted. Any hopes of an Israeli agreement to the creation of a Palestinian state in the West Bank and Gaza Strip in exchange for Arab recognition are fading fast. Despite massive international relief for the Kurdish refugees, and the safe-haven camps that have been set up, the Kurds no longer feel safe in Iraq. The outcome may be another conflict, for the Gulf War has not solved the underlying problems of the Middle East – religion, territory, politics and oil. The prospects for peace are not bright.

△ Kurds cross the Turkish border in a desperate attempt to flee from the brutal represssion of the Iraqi Army in April 1991. Thousands died on the road.

Middle Eastern countries

Bahrain: independent August 15, 1971
Capital: Manama
Constitution: Independent Sheikhdom
Population: 450,000 (including 150,000 foreigners)
Religion: Islam (Sunni 40 percent, Shi'ite 60 percent)

Egypt: independent February 28, 1922
Capital: Cairo
Constitution: Presidential Republic
Population: 52 million
Religion: Islam (Sunni 92 percent)

Iran: traditionally independent; known as Persia until March 21, 1935
Capital: Tehran
Constitution: Revolutionary Islamic Republic
Population: 50 million
Religion: Islam (Shi'ite 93 percent)

Iraq: independent October 3, 1932
Capital: Baghdad
Constitution: Socialist Presidential Republic (Ba'athist)
Population: 17.4 million
Religion: Islam (Sunni 40 percent, Shi'ite 50 percent)

Israel: independent May 14, 1948
Capital: Tel Aviv (Jerusalem is claimed as the capital, but is not recognized internationally)
Constitution: Parliamentary Democracy under titular president
Population: 4.2 million (currently being boosted by an influx of Soviet Jews)
Religion: Judaism (83 percent) Muslims (14 percent)

Jordan: independent March 22, 1946
Capital: Amman
Constitution: Constitutional Monarchy
Population: 2.8 million
Religion: Islam (Sunni 90 percent)

Kuwait: independent June 19, 1961
Capital: Kuwait City
Constitution: Independent Emirate
Population: 2.2 million (including 1.2 million foreigners) (Figures from before the Gulf War 1990-91)
Religion: Islam (Sunni 75 percent, Shi'ite 25 percent)

Lebanon: independent November 26, 1946
Capital: Beirut
Constitution: Presidential Parliamentary Democracy, with seats in the National Assembly divided between Christians and Muslims
Population: 2.7 million
Religion: Islam (57 percent with Shi'ite majority) and Christian (43 percent with Maronite majority)

Oman: independent December 20, 1951
Capital: Muscat
Constitution: Independent Sultanate
Population: 2 million
Religion: Islam (Ibadi 75 percent, Sunni 25 percent)

Qatar: independent September 1, 1971
Capital: Doha
Constitution: Independent Emirate
Population: 310,000 (including 225,000 foreigners)
Religion: Islam (Sunni 98 percent)

Saudi Arabia: independent September 23, 1932
Capital: Riyadh
Constitution: Kingdom
Population: 10 million
Religion: Islam (Sunni 85 percent, Shia 15 percent)

▽ The Sheraton Hotel in Doha, capital of Qatar, is a stunning symbol of oil wealth in the Gulf. The Gulf states have bought Western technology and expertise with their oil dollars.

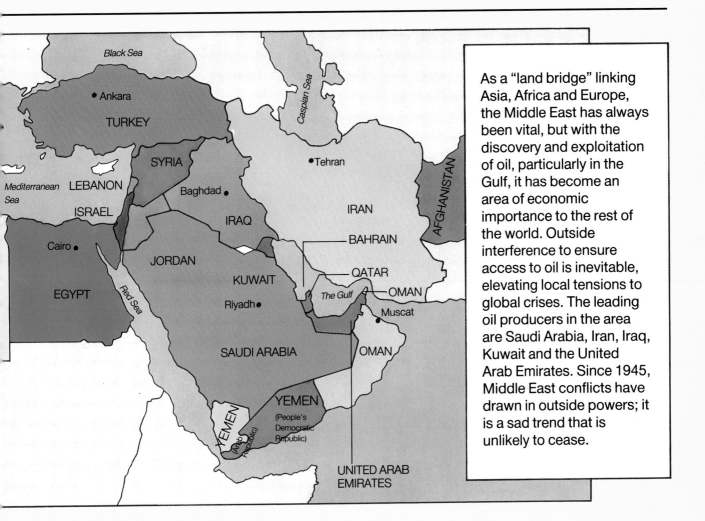

As a "land bridge" linking Asia, Africa and Europe, the Middle East has always been vital, but with the discovery and exploitation of oil, particularly in the Gulf, it has become an area of economic importance to the rest of the world. Outside interference to ensure access to oil is inevitable, elevating local tensions to global crises. The leading oil producers in the area are Saudi Arabia, Iran, Iraq, Kuwait and the United Arab Emirates. Since 1945, Middle East conflicts have drawn in outside powers; it is a sad trend that is unlikely to cease.

Syria: independent September 16, 1941
Capital: Damascus
Constitution: Presidential Republic (Ba'athist)
Population: 10.6 million
Religion: Islam (Sunni 75 percent, Shi'ite 10 percent)

United Arab Emirates: independent (as seven emirates) February 11, 1972
Capital: Abu Dhabi
Constitution: Federation of seven emirates (Abu Dhabi, Ajman, Dubai, Fujairah, Ras al-Khaimah, Sharjah and Umm al-Qaiwain) with presidency rotated
Population: 1.85 million
Religion: Islam (Sunni)

Yemen Arab Republic: independent 1911
Capital: Sana'a
Constitution: Presidential Republic
Population: 9.3 million
Religion: Islam (Shi'ite 50 percent, Sunni 50 percent)

People's Democratic Republic of Yemen: independent November 30, 1967
Capital: Aden
Constitution: Marxist Presidential Republic
Population: 2.4 million
Religion: Islam (Sunni)

On May 22, 1990 it was announced that the two Yemens had merged into one.

Affiliations
All the Middle Eastern countries are members of the United Nations. Most of the Arab countries are members of the Arab League. They include Bahrain, Egypt, Iraq, Jordan, Kuwait, Lebanon, Oman, Qatar, Saudi Arabia and the United Arab Emirates. Bahrain, Kuwait, Oman, Qatar, Saudi Arabia and the United Arab Emirates are members of the Gulf Cooperation Council. Iran, Iraq, Kuwait, Qatar, Saudi Arabia and the United Arab Emirates are all members of the Organization of Petroleum-Exporting Countries.

Weapons

The Middle East, with its profusion of wars, has been used by outside powers – particularly the United States and Soviet Union – as a "testing ground" for high-technology weapons. Their impact has often been significant, making the difference between victory and defeat for the side with the latest systems.

Air Weapons

Aircraft have always played a key role. A country that gains "air superiority" in war, defeating the enemy air force and flying unmolested through enemy skies, can observe enemy ground forces (using reconnaissance aircraft or pilotless "drones"), attack them (using bombers), and provide close support to its own ground units (using fighter bombers, ground attack aircraft or helicopters). In June 1967 the Israelis gained air superiority by a preemptive strike against Arab air forces, destroying many aircraft on their airfields, and went on to achieve remarkable victories on the ground. The US-led coalition did much the same against Iraq in early 1991, using its superior technology.

Such technology can take many forms. In the Gulf War, the Americans used F117A Stealth fighters to penetrate Iraqi radar screens – made possible by the angular shape and radar-absorbent materials of the aircraft. The 30-year-old B-52 bomber proved its worth, carrying 24,500 kg (54,000 lb) of high-explosives. The B-52s achieved accuracy by bombing on very precise, radar-assisted coordinates. The most devastating weapons were the so-called "smart" munitions, guided to their targets with unerring accuracy. If the target was "illuminated" with a beam of laser light (called a tracer), either from an aircraft or by soldiers on the ground, a laser-guided bomb could "ride the beam" to its destination.

Aircraft can be stopped, however. In October 1973 the Egyptians and Syrians deployed a sophisticated Soviet-designed air defense "umbrella" which initially proved effective. Heat-seeking surface-to-air missiles (SAMs), fired in response to radar warnings of air attack, flew toward incoming aircraft,

▽ The Lockheed F117A Stealth fighter was used by the Americans in the Gulf War, 1991. The aircraft has a small "radar signature," that reduces the enemy's ability to track it as it attacks.

▷ Patriot missiles proved effective against Scud missiles in 1991. Radars were the key, allowing Patriots to be fired toward incoming missiles before homing in using onboard radar systems.

aiming for the heat from the jet engines, while ZSU 23-4 radar-controlled multibarreled cannon put up a "wall" of shells that would destroy any aircraft flying through it. The Israelis countered this by jamming the radar frequencies and using heat flares, designed to divert the SAMs; in Lebanon in 1982 the Israelis also deployed remotely-piloted vehicles (RPVs) to trigger the radars so that electronic-warfare aircraft could monitor and jam the frequencies. Similar tactics were used by the allies in the Gulf in 1991.

Also in the Gulf, American-made Patriot SAMs found a new role, not against aircraft, but against Soviet-designed Scud missiles fired by Iraq into Israel and Saudi Arabia.

Land Weapons

Once air superiority has been gained, ground forces enjoy freedom from enemy air attack and are able to advance under their own air cover. Throughout the Middle East wars, the most important land weapon has been the tank, combining firepower, mobility and armor protection (although, in more recent conflicts, the attack helicopter, armed with missiles, has proved effective). In June 1967, it was Israeli tanks that took Sinai, advancing deep behind Egyptian lines to spread chaos and demoralization; in 1991 it was allied tanks that spearheaded the drive into southern Iraq.

Tanks, like aircraft, can be countered. In October 1973 Arab armies deployed Soviet-supplied AT-3 Sagger

△ A Challenger tank, equipped with 120mm gun and special Chobham "spaced" armor. Challengers were used by the British 1st Armored Division in the Gulf in 1991.

wired-guided antitank missiles which, once fired, could be directed onto a target by the operator by means of electronic signals passed down a wire trailing behind. More recently, antitank missiles have dispensed with the wire, homing in on laser beams or infrared emissions from the target. In all cases, the answer is to protect the tanks by making them part of an "all arms" team which includes infantry, artillery, engineers and ground attack aircraft, or by fitting them with better protective armor. Allied tanks in the Gulf War had "spaced" armor, so that an incoming antitank warhead exploded on an outer shell and did not penetrate to kill the crew. Israeli tanks in Lebanon in 1982 had "reactive" armor, where the outer shell exploded as soon as the warhead impacted, diverting the force of the hit.

Naval Weapons

Navies have not played a decisive role in Middle East wars, but their presence is often crucial to protect merchant shipping (such as oil tankers in the Iran-Iraq War), to provide support to ground forces close to coastal areas (such as U.S. battleships firing 16-inch shells in the northern Gulf in 1991), and to carry supplies. Few amphibious landings have been planned – some in Lebanon in 1982 and a feint landing outside Kuwait City by U.S. Marines in 1991 – but some of the weapons used have been dramatic. U.S. battleships in the Gulf War used Tomahawk cruise missiles against Iraq. During the same conflict, U.S. aircraft carriers acted as floating airfields, while allied minehunters cleared sea passages in the Gulf.

Nuclear weapons have not yet been used in the Middle East, although Israel is believed to possess them. Chemical weapons – particularly asphyxiating gas – have been used by the Iraqis against the Kurds and Iranians.

Chronology

632 AD Prophet Muhammad dies; new religion of Islam splits into Sunni and Shi'ite sects

1517-1918 Period of Ottoman (Turkish) rule over much of the Middle East

1869 Suez Canal opened.

1881 British take control of Egypt

1898 British seize control of Sudan

1914-18 World War I: Britain fights Turkey in Mesopotamia (Iraq), Palestine and Arabia

1916 Sykes-Picot Agreement by Britain and France over the division of the Ottoman Empire

1917 Balfour Declaration: Britain agrees to "view with favor" the creation of a Jewish homeland in Palestine

1920 Treaty of Sèvres breaks up the Ottoman Empire: Britain gains Palestine, Transjordan and Iraq, France gains "Greater Syria," all as mandates from the League of Nations; Lebanon created by the French as a separate, mainly Christian state

1932 Iraq gains full independence; Saudi Arabia formed

1936-39 Arab Revolt in Palestine against British rule

1939-45 World War II: Syria and Lebanon gain independence

1947 Britain gives notice of withdrawal from Palestine; UN votes for partition

1948 State of Israel created; attacked by five Arab powers but survives

1952 King Farouk of Egypt overthrown by the army

1954 Nasser seizes power in Egypt

1956 Nasser nationalizes the Suez Canal Company; Egypt is attacked by Britain, France and Israel

1958 United Arab Republic formed between Egypt and Syria. King Feisel of Iraq overthrown

1961 British troops sent to Kuwait to protect it against Iraq

1963 Ba'athists seize power in Syria

1964 PLO is formed

1967 Six-Day War: Israel attacks Egypt, Jordan and Syria to gain Sinai, the West Bank, Gaza Strip and Golan Heights; UN Resolution 242 demands withdrawal

1968 Ba'athists seize power in Iraq

1969-70 War of Attrition between Egypt and Israel

1970 King Hussein expels the PLO from Jordan.

1972 Palestinians murder Israeli athletes at Munich Olympics

1973 October War: Egypt and Syria attack Israel; Arab members of OPEC raise oil prices

1975 Algiers Accord between Iran and Iraq

1975-76 Civil War in Lebanon; Syria intervenes and occupies Beqa'a Valley

1978 Camp David agreement between Egypt and Israel

1979 Shah of Iran overthrown by fundamentalists loyal to Ayatollah Khomeini; American hostages taken in Tehran. Saddam Hussein seizes power in Iraq

1980 American operation to save hostages in Tehran fails

1980-88 Iran-Iraq War

1981 Israeli air strike on Iraqi nuclear reactor. Sadat of Egypt assassinated. American hostages released by Iran

1982 Operation Peace for Galilee: Israel invades southern Lebanon; PLO forced to leave Beirut; Palestinian families massacred in camps at Sabra and Chatilla

1988 5,000 inhabitants of the Kurdish village of Halabja are killed by Iraqi forces using chemical weapons

1990 Saddam Hussein of Iraq invades Kuwait; American-led coalition formed to oppose him (Desert Shield)

1991 US-led coalition attacks Iraq and liberates Kuwait (Desert Storm); civil war in Iraq ; up to 2.4 million Kurdish refugees try to flee Iraq; special safe-haven camps established for protection of Kurds

Glossary

Arab League is an international organization, formed in 1945 to promote political coordination, and economic and cultural links between all Arab states.

Ayatollah is the title given to a respected Islamic cleric of the Shi'ite sect, well versed in Islamic law.

Ba'ath is an Arab socialist party, formed in 1947 and dedicated to the promotion of Arab nationalism.

Coup is a forcible seizure of political power in a state, often using elements of the armed services.

Fundamentalism is a movement based on the strong belief that Muslims must return to the basic teachings of the *Koran*.

Gulf Cooperation Council (GCC) is an economic and political organization of six Arab states of the Gulf, formed in 1981.

Intifada is the Palestinian uprising against Israeli rule in the occupied territories of the West Bank and Gaza Strip.

Islam is the religion based on the *Koran* and on the reported sayings and acts of the Prophet Muhammad.

Jew is one of the Hebrew people and a believer in the religion of Judaism.

Jihad is a "holy war" declared by Muslims against non-believers or infidels.

Koran is the holy book of Islam.

Muslims see the *Koran* as containing the word of God, conveyed to mankind through the Prophet Muhammad.

Kurd is a member of a distinct ethnic and tribal group which straddles the borders between Iraq, Iran, Turkey, Syria and the Soviet Union.

League of Nations was an international organization, formed in 1919, through which disputes between nations could be settled without war. It was replaced by the United Nations.

Muslim is a follower of the Islamic faith.

Nationalism is the belief that individual communities or cultures – usually defined by a common language – should be independent.

October War was the conflict fought between Arab states (principally Egypt and Syria) and Israel in October 1973. Also known as the Yom Kippur War or Ramadan War.

Organization of Petroleum Exporting Countries (OPEC) is an international body representing 13 oil-producing states, formed in 1960.

Palestine Liberation Organization (PLO) is a political and military body, formed in 1964 to represent Palestinian Arabs.

Pan-Arabism is the belief that all Arabs should belong to one nation, not individual states.

Peace for Galilee was the Israeli attack on southern Lebanon in 1982, designed to remove the PLO threat to northern Galilee.

Preemptive Strike is a military term for a surprise attack, designed to hit your enemies before they attack you.

Shiaism is the Islamic sect which originally comprised the supporters of the Prophet Muhammad's cousin and son-in-law, Ali. Believers are known as Shi'ites.

Six-Day War was the conflict fought in June 1967 between Israel and its Arab neighbors, in which the Israelis seized Sinai, the West Bank, the Gaza Strip and the Golan Heights.

Sunni is the Islamic sect which originally included followers of the Prophet Muhammad's father-in-law, Abu Bakr.

Superpower is a country which has immense economic, political and military (including nuclear) strength. It refers to the United States and Soviet Union.

United Nations (UN) is an international organization, formed in 1945 to replace the League of Nations as a forum for settling disputes between countries. Resolutions passed by the UN Security Council are binding on all member states.

War of Attrition was a conflict fought in 1969-70 by Egypt and Israel along the Suez Canal.

Zionism is an extreme form of Jewish nationalism, dedicated to a strong Jewish state.

Index

Photographic Credits:
Front cover and pages 2-3, 4-5, 6-7, 7, 12-13 top and bottom, 14-15, 15, 16-17, 17, 18-19, 18, 19, 21, 22-23, 22, 23, 26-27, 26, 27, 28-29, 29 bottom, 30 and 32 left and right: Frank Spooner Pictures; page 5: Mary Evans Picture Library; pages 8-9 top, 10-11, 24-25 bottom and 29 top: Topham

Picture Source; pages 8-9 bottom, 12, 20-21 and 24-25 top: Popperfoto; page 33: British Crown Copyright/ MOD reproduced with the permission of the Controller of Her Britannic Majesty's Stationary Office; back cover: United Nations Relief and Works Agency For Palestine Refugees In The Near East.

PRINTED IN BELGIUM BY
proost
INTERNATIONAL BOOK PRODUCTION